Bakeries

Teaching Tips

Purple Level 8

This book focuses on the phonemes **/ie/ea/**.

Before Reading

- Discuss the title. Ask readers what they think the book will be about. Have them support their answer.
- Discuss the book's focused phonemes. Explain that /ie/ has two main sounds: long /i/ and long /e/, and /ea/ has three different sounds: long /e/, short /e/, and long /a/. Give examples of each.

Read the Book

- Encourage readers to read independently, either aloud or silently to themselves.
- Prompt readers to break down unfamiliar words into units of sound and string the sounds together to form the words. Then, ask them to look for context clues to see if they can figure out what these words mean. Discuss new vocabulary to confirm meaning.
- Urge readers to point out when each focused phonics phoneme appears in the text. What sound does it make?

After Reading

- Ask readers comprehension questions about the book. How do bakers do their job?
- Encourage readers to think of other words with the /ie/ or /ea/ phoneme. On a separate sheet of paper, have them write the words into columns by sound.

© 2024 Booklife Publishing
This edition is published by arrangement with Booklife Publishing.

North American adaptations © 2024 Jump!
5357 Penn Avenue South
Minneapolis, MN 55419
www.jumplibrary.com

Decodables by Jump! are published by Jump! Library.
All rights reserved. No part of this book may be reproduced in any form without written permission from the publisher.

Library of Congress Cataloging-in-Publication Data is available at www.loc.gov or upon request from the publisher.

ISBN: 979-8-88996-888-7 (hardcover)
ISBN: 979-8-88996-889-4 (paperback)
ISBN: 979-8-88996-890-0 (ebook)

Photo Credits

Images are courtesy of Shutterstock.com. With thanks to Getty Images, Thinkstock Photo and iStockphoto. Cover – Krakenimages.com. 3 – Valentin Valkov, Stepan Bormotov, Naruedom Yaempongsa, Olhastock, VictorH11, seksan wangjaisuk, SeDmi. 4–5 – Kues, Viktoriia Hnatiuk. 6–7 – Daisy Daisy, Tyler Olson. 8–9 – BongkarnGraphic, PeopleImages.com - Yuri A. 10–11 – casanisa, Natalya_Maisheva. 12–13 – Luciavonu, Maurizio Milanesio. 14–15 – Melnikov Sergey, Monkey Business Images. 16 – Shutterstock.

Which of these items do you think you might find in a bakery?

A baker is a person who makes bread, cakes, pastries, and other baked goods. They may sell their goods to shops or display them in their own bakeries.

Bakers have to get up before most people so that they have time to set up before people come to get breakfast. They may wake up while it is still dark.

It is important for bakers to have good hygiene. They keep their hands, tools, and worktops clean while they bake. They may wear aprons and tie their hair up too.

Bakers must keep track of what is in each baked good so that people with allergies do not get ill. They use labels so that people know what is in each item.

To get a perfect bake, bakers have to use exact amounts. They cannot just add random amounts of yeast or eggs. If they do, the baked goods will not come out right.

Mixing correctly is important too. If bakers mix a batter for a long time instead of giving it a brief fold, they may end up with a flat cake.

While some baked goods can be made in a short amount of time, bread needs quite a while. Bakers have to wait for bread to rise before they bake it. This is called proofing.

To make bread rise, bakers add yeast to the mix. When the mix is set aside in a place that is not too cold, it will expand to fill the bowl.

After it is proofed and shaped, bread goes on a tray and is baked. Bread expands as it bakes, so bakers make sure to spread out the pieces of dough so that they do not stick when they rise.

Bakers can tell when bread is baked well. It turns gold and gives off a pleasant smell. They let it cool on racks.

At some bakeries, you can get tier cakes. These are cakes that have a number of stacked layers. They may be decorated with lots of flowers and berries.

Think ahead to the next time you are going to bake. What will you make? You could make a pie, a pizza crust, gingerbread cookies, and more!

Say the name of each object below. Is the "ie" in each a long /e/ sound or a long /i/ sound?

shield

flies

cried

lilies